IMAGES OF ENGLAND

CENTRAL
LEICESTER

IMAGES OF ENGLAND

CENTRAL
LEICESTER

STEPHEN BUTT

TEMPUS

To my wife, Linda

Frontispiece: All Saints' church on Highcross Street. A building with Norman origins now surrounded by Victorian and later industrial architecture.

First published 2005

Tempus Publishing Limited
The Mill, Brimscombe Port,
Stroud, Gloucestershire, GL5 2QG
www.tempus-publishing.com

British Library Cataloguing in Publication Data.
A catalogue record for this book is available from the British Library.

ISBN 0 7524 3674 0

Typesetting and origination by Tempus Publishing Limited.
Printed in Great Britain.

Contents

Acknowledgements

My grateful thanks for permission to reproduce photographs in this book and for providing advice and information go to Ben Beazley, Chris Bell of the Tommy Atkins Society, Victor Berridge, Gwynneth Brookes, John Burrows, Neville Chadwick and Keith Dickens all of the Leicester Civic Society, M. Ford, Edwin W. Green, Tony Green, G. Jordan, Roger Lovell, Mrs Millward, David Morris, Janet Nolan, Jeremy Perkins, Nigel Tout, Stuart Marbrooke, Paul Vyse-Widdicombe, K. Wigley and Barbara Wilson.

Introduction

The history of Leicester spans 2,000 years, from the establishment of a Roman military garrison at the intersection of two important roads to the large bustling multicultural city of the present day and forms an almost unbroken narrative. The photographic record covers no more than 160 years, but it reflects times of great change and accelerated development.

The Romans occupied Leicester for 360 years. Their influence on the layout of the medieval town can still be seen today in the grid-like structure of the streets in the area of St Martin's and Greyfriars. The Danes controlled the town for just forty years but their presence is reflected in the names of the streets spreading outwards from the area of the clock tower: Churchgate, Belgrave Gate, Humberstone Gate and Gallowtree Gate. The suffix 'gate' being the Danish word for 'street' or 'road'.

The city's motto *semper eadem* (always the same) has regularly attracted comment. To some observers Leicester is a city that seldom changes and is somewhat content not to aspire to great buildings or dramatic projects. It is however, a place of great diversity, and some of its former and present citizens – from the father of the excursion holiday, Thomas Cook, to the creator of diarist Adrian Mole, Sue Townsend – have given the city a place in history and on the world stage. In the early twentieth century a Jewish community grew up in the Highfields district, and after 1945, Polish and Latvian refugees moved into this area. In the 1950s West Indians moved into the city, and a decade later, Asian families came to Leicester, their numbers increasing in the 1970s when forced to leave Uganda by Idi Amin. More recently, people from Somalia, Ghana and Kenya have formed communities in the city. The influence of these many different cultures is reflected in the shops and the buildings of twenty-first-century Leicester.

A fair number of household names from the business and commercial world came into existence through initially trading in Leicester. Curry's began in Belgrave Gate as a bicycle manufacturer and is now part of the major electrical retail group that includes Dixons and PC World; Wilkinson's, the household goods chain, began trading as a small family business in Upper Charnwood Street in 1930. Fox's Glacier Mints, Walker's crisps and Everard's ales are all products known worldwide, and 'made in Leicester'.

Leicester has few buildings that can be described as dramatic, but there are many interesting structures that add to the character of the city. The Town Hall is not as grand as the municipal buildings in many cities, but it is a warm and beautifully balanced building that works well in its context. The city has no obvious focal point other than its much-loved Victorian clock tower (which in fact stands *outside* the eastern boundaries of the old town), but it has a remarkable tree-lined New Walk right at its heart, as well as the great expanse of Abbey Park. In the twenty-first century many new buildings are changing the skyline, such as the National Space Centre, and the innovative Queen's Building of De Montfort University. Many others are being refurbished and converted, giving a new role for redundant churches and chapels, the factories and mills of the last industrial era and even the former city police station in Charles Street.

Buildings are often described as having 'character', but surely the essence of a city is in its people. In this book are people from many different walks of life, some famous and others unknown. They provide the context for the buildings; they populate the shop-lined streets, relax in the parks or are shown posing proudly or shyly for the photographer.

One can now only imagine the nature of the town as it was in the years following the departure of the Romans, an atmosphere of decay and desolation. Perhaps a similar atmosphere pervaded those Leicester streets of empty houses awaiting slum clearance in the 1950s and 1960s. It is certainly present in the old textile factories awaiting refurbishment. This collection of photographs includes a number of those buildings which appear, at least for the time being, to have lost their soul and purpose; but even those in a most ruinous state often speak of past glories.

A variety of different photographers have produced the images in this compilation. The earliest photographs date to the latter half of the nineteenth century when photography on location – as opposed to studio shots – was still a novelty. Some of these early images record significant events in the history of Leicester such as the demolition of the old borough gaol, or the very short period of time when the church of St Stephen could be seen next to the new frontage of the Midland Railway station on London Road. Other early images are remarkably personal in capturing fleeting moments in the history of a family, a wedding, the return of a soldier from the battlefield or a fondly remembered day out. Some of the later images continue with the purpose of recording the changing face of the city while others point up the contrasts of architecture or style.

During the years covered by the photographs in this collection, the town of Leicester became a city and gained a bishop and a cathedral. The General Hospital was opened, the horse-drawn trams were converted to electricity, the first purpose-built cinema in the town – the Electric Theatre in High Street – opened to the public and the first council house was built.

A familiar debate among archivists and historians is the question of what should be saved of our past. Many photographs have survived simply by accident or good fortune, but now provide a fascinating glimpse of a society or community which no longer exists. The new digital age, offering the facility for immediate deletion raises new considerations, as perhaps future compilers will inherit only an edited and digitally adjusted picture of the past.

Stephen Butt
June 2005

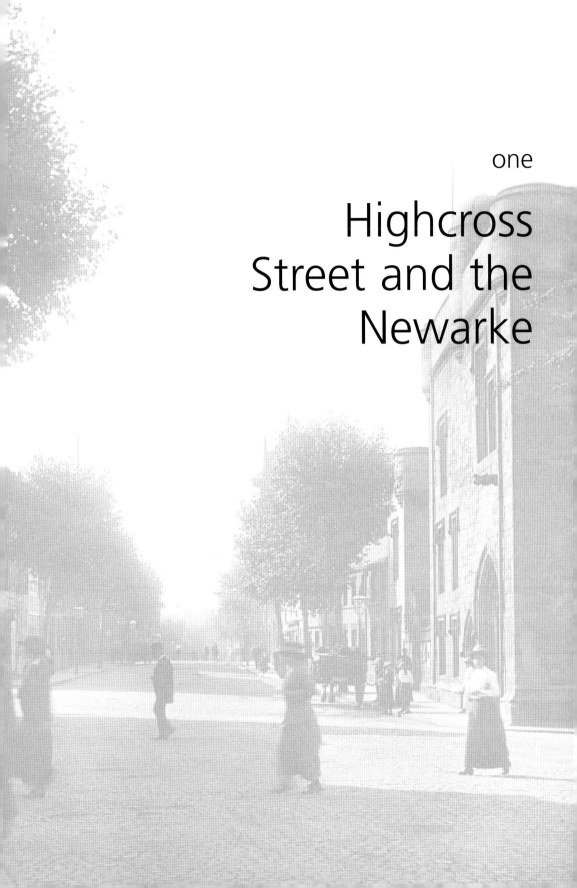

one

Highcross
Street and the
Newarke

The Newarke was a small district beside the east bank of the River Soar outside the old walled area of the town. It was formerly occupied by the College of St Mary founded by Henry, Earl of Lancaster in 1330 and included a church of grand scale. All that exists today is a part of the hospital now used by the administration of De Montfort University. The Magazine Gateway is one of two ancient entrances to the Newarke to have survived. The 3rd Earl of Leicester built it in about 1410, and, as it lacks a portcullis, it would seem that its principal role was to impress rather than to be defensive. The upper floor is divided into two large rooms with a large fireplace on one side, reached by a spiral staircase. The central ring road development of the 1960s left the Gateway isolated, the only access being by pedestrian subway. This view is from inside the precincts of the Newarke looking through the Gateway towards Newarke Street. The Drill Hall on the right, which was built in 1894 as the headquarters of the Territorial units of the Leicestershire Regiment, was demolished in the 1950s.

Opposite: Oxford Street was originally the approach for merchants and traders to the South Gate of the medieval town. Over several centuries, as the axis of the town moved towards the Eastern boundary and the area of the Saturday Market, this route, including Southgate Street and Highcross Street, became less important. There is a sense of peace in this Edwardian photograph looking south from the junction with Newarke Street.

The factory chimney in the distance is a reminder of the textile industry that occupied central areas of Leicester in the nineteenth and early twentieth centuries. Taken in around 1900, this view of the Magazine Gateway includes part of the later Drill Hall extensions on the Newarke side. The chimney belonged to one several small factories located on the northern side of Newarke Street.

The Hawthorn Building of the College of Art and Design was built in the Newarke in 1897 by S. Perkins Pick at the cost of £25,000. This early view, with the spire of St Mary de Castro in the distance, shows the building before it was extended in 1909. In 1927, with further extensions, it became the Colleges of Art and Technology. In the basement of the building are the only surviving remains of the church of the Newarke College. In 1969, the colleges merged to form Leicester Polytechnic which acquired university status in 1989. The Hawthorn Building is now the home of the Faculty of Applied Science at De Montfort University.

Above: The River Soar bounds the Newarke to the east. This view from the Newarke Bridge across the area to the north-east, unimpeded by the later construction of Victorian factories and other buildings on what is now the campus of De Montfort University, shows the spires of St Mary de Castro and St Martin and dates from the early nineteenth century. The bridge is now a Grade II listed building.

Right: The buildings and the landscape that make up the area now known as Castle Park have a timeless quality, but interesting comparisons can be made between this photograph, taken at the end of the eighteenth century, and the same view today. The Turret Gate was built in 1422-23 and connects the Newarke with the castle enclosures. It is claimed that the witch, Black Annis, lies in wait beside the gateway for those crossing the boundary at midnight.

No. 55 Highcross Street was typical of many imposing buildings that lined this street in its heyday. Standing on the corner of Free School Lane, this building of quiet elegance served several purposes in its time, including the location of undertakers Arthur Earp & Sons.

No. 44 Highcross Street stood on the corner of Highcross and St Nicholas Streets overlooking the market site at the High Cross, and in the 1950s was the home of the health food stores of John Wood & Co. Ltd. The site is now a car park.

Right: No. 56 Highcross Street. This road was the axis of medieval Leicester and its line emphasises the symmetrical nature of the underlying Roman plan. Running from the North Gate to the South Gate, the street was Leicester's original High Street. The town's High Cross was situated where Highcross Street crossed the modern High Street (formerly Swinesmarket) and St Nicholas Street, the location of a busy market until the middle of the nineteenth century.

This section of Highcross Street, from Peacock Lane to High Street, is now known as St Nicholas Place. To the right of this photograph, taken in the 1970s, are Guildhall Lane, the former Wyggeston School, the Guildhall and the cathedral. The derelict corner building is now a thriving restaurant, its façade having been recently restored, but the former Wathes building on the left has been demolished, as has the building further along Guildhall Lane opposite the Guildhall.

Opposite, below: Demolition of the old borough (county) gaol at the junction of Freeschool Lane and Highcross Street, *c.* 1880. A borough gaol had existed in Highcross Street from as early as 1297. A new prison was built at the corner of Highcross Street and Causeway Lane in about 1614, rebuilt in 1793, and demolished in 1847. In 1824, the corporation planned a new prison and purchased land adjacent to the existing building, but the project was halted due to public protest. In 1835, the corporation bought the nearby county gaol on the corner of Freeschool Lane instead. This building had also been altered considerably and become redundant when the new county prison in Welford Road – still in use today – had opened. The cost to the corporation of the purchase and necessary alterations was enormous. When the Prison Commissioners took over the prison in 1878 they closed it but the building was bought back by the borough and demolished in 1880.

The former T.H. Wathes store was built in the middle of the nineteenth century as a shop and warehouse for cheese merchants Swain and Latchmore. T.H. Wathes ran a retail store in nearby High Street, later expanding to take over this building. Dr John Barclay, in a lecture to the Leicester Literary and Philosophical Society in 1857 noted, 'new buildings of a commercial character are very numerous ... improvement in this class of buildings is most marked... Almost the first step towards improvement was in the shop and warehouses of Messrs Swain & Latchmore in Southgate Street. The front is here decorated with coloured encaustic tiles let into the brickwork. I do not know that this is a style to be followed, but I mention it as a step in the right direction'. Dr Barclay was not a native and may therefore be forgiven for giving the wrong street name! The tiles and most of the roof slates from this building were saved and incorporated into the new BBC Centre, built in its place, and opened in Spring 2005.

This road junction, insignificant today in terms of the city centre's traffic system, is close to the early intersection of the Highcross Street and the Roman Fosse Way. This photograph is of the narrow Guildhall Lane with the Guildhall itself just in view between the cathedral and the twentieth-century extensions to the former Wyggeston School. The office and school printing suppliers, Block and Anderson, traded from the corner building until the late 1950s and their name can still be read above the first floor windows.

Right: The inner courtyard of the medieval Guildhall, originally the home of the Gild of Corpus Christi, was built around 1380. Religious gilds played an important role in English life in the fourteenth and fifteenth centuries. Corpus Christi – established by nine burgesses and four Normans from the castle administration in 1343 – was the most influential of the gilds that existed at that time. After the Reformation, the Gild was dissolved and its property transferred to the Crown but the borough was permitted its use it as a meeting place.

Below: It seems incredible now that, at one time, the corporation considered the demolition of the Guildhall. In its long history, this building has served as a police station, public library, records office and town hall. In more recent years, the building has been treated with greater respect, including sensitive conservation, and is now closely associated with the adjacent Cathedral Visitors' Centre. It is also a museum under the management of Leicester City Council.

William Albert Green sketched this picture of the Castle Gate and the preceding image of the Guildhall. A Birmingham artist, born in 1907, he began drawing in his teenage years, using pencil and water color and turned to pen and ink working. He continued until a few years before his death despite poor eyesight. He made pencil sketches on location (travelling by bicycle or public transport) which he later traced onto paper, completing the drawing in ink and a fine pen. He specialised in historic buildings of the Midland counties, mainly in the Birmingham and Warwickshire areas but also in Shropshire, his home in later years. There are just a few examples of his work of buildings in Leicester. Green sold the drawings mainly to family and friends but later a Midland omnibus company began using his pictures to illustrate tour guides, and his status as an artist grew. Later his work appeared in *The Birmingham Weekly Post* illustrating the weekly rambling article by John Hingle and in other Midlands newspapers including *The Sunday Mercury*, *The Birmingham Post* and *The Birmingham Mail*. The drawings appeared in magazines and, famously, on the back of England's Glory matchboxes.

Above: Earliest parts of the castle date to the twelfth century but the hall was used as a court of law from the times of the Earls of Leicester until the late twentieth century. The broken windows in this nineteenth-century photograph of the castle frontage suggest a period of neglect. The surviving hall has been heavily restored on several occasions, most recently in 1856 under the supervision of the county surveyor William Parsons.

Right: This peaceful courtyard between the castle and the church of St Mary de Castro belies its former role as a place of execution. The castle's origins date back almost seven centuries to King Henry III who gave his son, Edmund, the estates forfeited by rebellious barons. In 1265, he gave Edmund lands that had belonged to Simon de Montfort, Earl of Leicester, and later lands taken from Robert Ferrers, Earl of Derby. In 1267 his inheritance gained the name of Lancaster and Edmund was given the county, the honour, the castle and title, Earl of Lancaster. These lands are still retained by the Duchy today.

Part of the attractive complex of buildings in the vicinity of the Castle, Castle House (or the Judge's Lodgings) beside the church of St Mary de Castro that provided accommodation for judges attending the county court sittings.

Opposite, below: Thomas Baskerville, who visited Leicester in about 1675, referred to the Jewry Wall as 'an old piece of Building which they call Janus's Temple'. By the end of the seventeenth century, as recorded in the records of the Borough of Leicester, these Roman remains were known as the Jury Wall. More accurately the structure is part of the palaestra or exercise hall of the Roman baths. These extensive remains were excavated by Kathleen Kenyon in 1933-36. The ancient church of St Nicholas, the builders of which made use of considerable quantities of Roman material, stands nearby, and this photograph is of the side of the Jewry Wall facing the west end of the church. A gap of just 12ft separates the two structures.

John of Gaunt most certainly rode through this gateway to his castle, as did Henry VI in 1426. Simon de Montfort would have been familiar with it and Geoffrey Chaucer, who was attached to the retinue of John of Gaunt, probably visited from time to time as well.

In the 1960s, when this photograph was taken, the building at the corner of two of Leicester's medieval streets was in poor repair. However, despite opposition from some conservationists, Leicester City Council created the St Martin's shopping precinct, which has resulted in renewed prosperity for the little shops in the area now known as Leicester Lanes.

two

Entertainment

On 14 August 1967, the Marine Offences Bill came into force and made the operation of pirate radio stations illegal on the British mainland and inside its territorial waters. Within a matter of weeks the BBC opened Britain's first mainland local radio station, in Leicester. Members of the Free Radio Association saw a political connection between the two events and mounted a protest on 8 November 1967 just minutes before BBC Radio Leicester went on air. The Association believed that a network of local stations operated only by the BBC was not a suitable substitute for the pirates. The scaffolding behind the protestors in Lower Hill Street was in preparation for the building of Crown House, a high-rise building, which was to accommodate government agencies including the Department of Health and Social Security. The building became vacant in the 1990s.

Opposite, above: At the BBC, dark suits were still evidently all the rage in 1967, which was also the year of flower power, psychedelia and Sergeant Pepper! In the studios of BBC Radio Leicester on the eighth floor of Epic House in Charles Street, listening to the opening moments are, from left to right: the Postmaster General, Rt Hon. Edward Short MP, Director General of the BBC, Sir Hugh Carleton Greene, Lord Mayor of Leicester, Ald. Sir Mark Henig and BBC Radio Leicester's first manager, Maurice Ennals.

Opposite, below: The famous concert organ, built by Stephen Taylor & Sons Ltd and a gift of Alfred Corah of the famous Leicester textile family, dominates the stage at the De Montfort Hall. On stage are amateur and professional entertainers and musicians at a concert marking the tenth anniversary of BBC Local Radio in November 1977. The organ was unveiled at a recital on 18 February 1914 and is the last surviving example of a Taylor concert organ. It was fully refurbished in 2004.

The De Montfort Hall soon after completion in 1913. The venue has seen a range of entertainments, from wrestling to ballet, and from pantomime to promenade concerts. The young Michael Tippett became convinced that his career was in music when he heard the Leicester Symphony Orchestra perform here, conducted by Malcolm Sargent, his music teacher at Stamford Grammar School. Years later, Sir Michael returned to conduct the Leicestershire Schools Symphony Orchestra in a performance of his oratorio *A Child of our Time*.

By the time Al Jolson was first heard in Leicester's picture palaces singing 'Sonny Boy', the days of the silent cinema were already numbered. It was certainly the swansong for the Lyric, or Knighton, cinema in Clarendon Park Road. The cinema operated from about 1913 in the former Liberal Hall but it never converted to sound and closed in the early 1920s. When this photograph was taken in the 1980s, the building had been used as a warehouse and was for sale. It has since been renovated and is now home to the Leicester Chinese Christian Church.

Opposite the A-1 Meat Company's premises was Lief's pawn shop, an establishment central to the lives of many residents of Wharf Street. It was built originally as two separate shops (by Isaac Barradale in 1880) numbered 27a and 27b. This numbering was necessary because part of the building occupies the original access to the Cricket Ground, which lay behind that side of Wharf Street. When the ground was sold for development, the original No. 27 was demolished, and the new building, partly across the entrance to the old ground, became two properties. Leicester's only surviving Victorian theatre is on the corner next door. There is little to indicate its presence except the façade above the first floor windows with theatre-style motifs. The building began life as the Gladstone Hotel in 1862 and originally had a third storey. It was not a success and became a meeting hall for religious groups and the Ragged School and by 1880 was the Gladstone Music Hall, or Gladstone Vaults. In 1883 Sam Torr, owner of the nearby Green Man

pub, bought it and re-opened it as the Gaiety Palace of Varieties. Sam had earlier associations with Joseph Carey Merrick, the Elephant Man, who had written to him from the Leicester Workhouse in 1884, suggesting that he might use his disfigurement to some monetary advantage on the stage. Merrick had been born nearby at 50 Lee Street. A plaque commemorates the claimed appearance of him on the stage. Torr's venture failed to prosper and was under new management in 1895 as the New Empire Theatre of Varieties. Perhaps it was attracting the 'wrong sort of clientele' at this time because the adjacent building, later to be Lief's pawnshop, may have been a brothel. In 1922 it became The Empire picture house and showed films until the 1940s eventually falling into disrepair in the 1950s. Today the building is home to a thriving motor factoring business, but now there is little to remind us of the time when it played a central role in the life of Wharf Street.

The first theatre proper in Leicester was built in 1750. In 1799 the subscribers chose to build a new theatre, designed by John Johnson, which opened in 1800, and this was demolished in 1836 to make way for the construction of the Theatre Royal. Whereas Johnson's theatre faced Hotel Street, the Theatre Royal, occupying the same site, faced the busier Horsefair Street. The building had a classical façade, with Ionic columns above an arcade that stood over the street. For many years, the well-known John Windley was the manager. Many famous names, both of local and national relevance, were associated with the theatre. Local theatre entrepreneur Frederick Hames worked here as a mask-maker from 1920. Wilkie Collins' own adaptation of *The Woman in White* was staged here in August 1870.

Above: Older residents of Leicester still talk of the Theatre Royal in Horsefair Street with affection. It was built in 1836 on the site of an earlier theatre and was the city's only theatre between 1849 and 1877. The design was the result of a partnership between Samuel Beazley and the Leicester architect and surveyor William Parsons.

Right: The Pageant of Leicester in 1932 was, by any standards, a major event. Organised by Frank Lascelles, a cast of thousands re-enacted scenes from Leicester's history from the Romans to the opening of Abbey Park in 1882. Hugh Goodacre wrote a special song, put to music by local musician Walter Groocock. Designs for the colourful floats still survive in Leicester's archives. The Lord Mayor of London opened Charles Street, a bypass route to ease the congestion around the Clock Tower, en route to the pageant.

THE PAGEANT OF LEICESTER AND INDUSTRIAL EXHIBITION JUNE 16TH-25TH 1932

The Odeon cinema in Queen Street pictured here in 1994, opened in 1938, one of many created by Oscar Deutsch. Older residents of the city remember seeing the massive oak beams, which support the roof, being transported through the city to the site, just off Charles Street. The first film was *A Slight Case of Murder* starring Edward G. Robinson and Jean Bryan. The auditorium accommodated 2,182 people and was the last large family cinema to be erected in Leicester. After a period of neglect the building has been restored and is now a multi-purpose banqueting and entertainment centre.

Opposite, above: The Coronation of Queen Elizabeth II in 1953 was the first to be watched by a television audience but across the country communities organised their own entertainments to mark the occasion. In New Parks in Leicester, the Lord Mayor (and former MP for Leicester North-West) Barnett Janner crowned the New Parks beauty queen. The location is Aikman Avenue on the New Parks Estate.

Opposite, below: When the Saffron Lane Sports Centre opened, it ranked as one of the finest facilities of its kind. It includes a cycle track with floodlighting and accommodation for 2,000 people. As seen in this photograph from the 1970s, cycling remains an important aspect of city life, but ironically Leicester's best known unsolved murder also involved a bicycle – the infamous 'green bicycle' mystery of 1919.

In February 1984 Princess Diana visited Leicester and her engagements included a visit to the factory of textile manufacturer T. W. Kempton on Belgrave Gate. Kempton's was once a market leader in the textile industry alongside such other local manufacturers as Faire Brothers and Corah's. No longer a mass producer, the Kempton name remains in Leicester as a supplier and manufacturer of technically advanced, high performance clothing and armour protection equipment.

Leicester's Little Theatre can be seen in this photograph of Dover Street – the van is parked outside its box office entrance. The white façade opposite is the Dover Castle public house and facing the end of the street, in Granby Street, is Balmoral House. The theatre building was constructed originally in 1823 as a chapel for a breakaway group of Baptists and was used later as a meeting place for the Independent Order of Rechabites.

three
People and Places

A studio portrait of Samuel Goodwin, his wife Minnie and their children Bernard and Hilda in 1909. Trade directories of the period show a considerable number of studio photographers working in Leicester at the beginning of the twentieth century. Over 100 are listed in local historian Jonathan Wilshere's pamphlet of Leicester photographers working before 1900.

A wedding photograph of 1932 from the archives of Leicester's Nolan family. The bride and bridegroom are Nora and Bernard. The bride's father, Alfred, is on the far right. Rather than using an outdoor location, the photographer, probably more accustomed to studio work, has constructed a makeshift internal backdrop for the study.

Above, left: Those occasions when serving officers were able to return home during the First World War were savoured. This photograph of Alfred Perry, his wife Jennie and daughters Nora, Grace, Irene and Sarah was taken in 1915 at their Belgrave home. All daughters later worked as machinists in Leicester's hosiery industry.

Above, right: When Alfred Perry left the army he continued to wear a uniform – as a postman. He is seen here outside his home in around 1930.

Left: A family visit to a terraced house in Leicester in about 1897. The precise location of 'Hazeldean' (engraved above the doorway) and the significance of the event are now lost but it is an unusually candid photograph – all seem oblivious of the photographer.

Above left: The earliest portrait photographers regarded their work as an extension of painted portraiture and this picture from 1873 of two smartly dressed boys is more 'candid' in nature than some other posed studies of the time. It has not been 'cropped' but is exactly as it was taken by the Victorian photographer. They appear to be the same two boys that appear with their family in the portrait over the page.

Above right: Peter Barrington and his dog Judy borrowed two stools from the bar of the Fox and Hounds in Humberstone Road to see over the wall of the pub yard in around 1948. Peter's grandfather, and later his father, ran the pub from 1936.

A group of gentlemen on an outing to Bradgate Park in 1873 – their dress seems strangely out of place for the rural setting. This rocky outcrop is still a landmark in the park, just inside the Cropston entrance. Charles Bennion gave the land, a former deer park, to the people of Leicestershire in 1928. Bennion was a director of the British United Shoe Company, so perhaps this picture records a staff outing from that company.

Right: A delightful portrait from the same photographer. A 'natural' pose but great care has been taken to produce a balanced composition. There is a timeless quality about this study, which dates to the last years of the nineteenth century.

Below: Another beautifully composed image. This late Victorian photographer has forsaken his studio to tackle portraiture on location and it is evident that he had studied the work of painters of the time. The location is Aylestone Meadows.

Left: A group of portraits follow from a Leicester photographer of the late nineteenth century. These images were recorded as lantern slides and are presumably of the photographer's family and relatives.

Below: The family by a river.

A little girl poses in a backyard wearing her smart winter clothes.

Three brothers and a moving story. Pte Cyril Hill (right) who served with the 9th Battalion of the Leicester Regiment died in action on 3 May 1917, aged nineteen years. His brother, Pte Shirley Hill (left), served with the 6th Battalion of the Seaforth Highlanders and died on 21 March 1916, aged nineteen years. Their younger brother, Arthur, survived them both but tragically died at the age of four, two years after this photograph was taken.

A close-up portrait of the mother from the family group above (page 40).

A close-up study of the father.

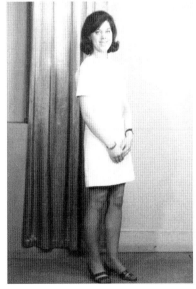

Above: Five sisters (from left to right: Margaret, Geraldine, Kathleen, Mabel and Olive Sharp) proudly display the many prizes they had won in skipping competitions. The family lived formerly in Swadlincote but this photograph was taken in about 1910 after they had moved to Leicester.

Right: Possibly the most easily defined fashion styles since the Second World War were those of the 1960s. This photograph, taken in studios in Granby Street, Leicester, shows young Gwynneth Brooks in the typical fashion of her teenage years. The date is August 1968.

Leicester City stars of the 1980s (from the left), Gary Lineker, Steve Lynex, John O'Neill and Andy Peake with BBC reporter Nigel Kay (centre) and fans, Stephanie and Elizabeth. This was the winning line-up under manager Jock Wallace in the 1980/81 season. Local lad Gary is regarded as one of the world's foremost strikers and many regard this season as the one in which his career first blossomed. Gary became a Freeman of the City in 1995 and the north stand at the new Walker's Stadium, opened in July 2002, is named after him.

David Gower, the golden boy of Leicestershire County Cricket, pictured in the 1970s at Grace Road with radio reporter Dennis Coath. Gower played for Leicestershire from 1977 to 1989 and captained in 1984–86 and 1988–89. His achievement of 8,231 runs in test matches makes him England's second highest-ever run scorer in test match history. His stylish play took him to eighteen test match centuries and thirty-two tests as captain of England. He was awarded the OBE in 1992 and retired from the game in 1993.

four
Transport

In 1969, the viaducts carrying the Great Central Railway's tracks into the station from the south were demolished. When it was constructed, the line altered Leicester's skyline forever, as the tracks were carried across part of the oldest areas of the town on viaducts. Some of the arches remain today, home to a number of small businesses, particularly in the area of Frog Island.

Opposite, above: The Great Central Railway was cut through Leicester during the last years of the nineteenth century providing a new route from Sheffield, south to London. Unlike the Midland Railway route, which was laid down before much of the land adjacent to it, on the southern boundaries of the town, was developed, the construction of the GCR required the demolition of a considerable number of buildings, residential and commercial, in the heart of the medieval town. This photograph of the frontage of the Great Central Station in Great Central Street was taken in 1967.

Opposite, below: The Great Central Railway's golden era was relatively short-lived. The reduction of its services began in 1960 when the daytime expresses between Manchester and London were withdrawn. Entire sections of the route were closed to passenger traffic in the late 1960s and the final section through Leicester, from Nottingham to Rugby, was closed in 1969.

A scene of desolation at the Great Central Railway's south goods yard, from the Upperton Road bridge, following the line's closure in 1969. On the horizon can be seen the spire of St Mary de Castro in the heart of the Newarke area. Most of this area has been since been redeveloped.

Bicycles are synonymous with Leicester and a number of technical developments in cycling have been made here, including this 'recumbent' bicycle pictured here in about 1940. The electrical retailer Curry's began its life in Leicester as a manufacturer of bicycles. Welding and other skills had been learned by the original Mr Curry while he was an apprentice in the steam engine house of the Corah textile factory at St Margaret's.

Arguably the most impressive approach to Leicester's city centre is the route of London Road towards the Clock Tower. This is the view from near the junction of London Road with Granville Road and St Alban's Road in the early years of the twentieth century. The Marquess of Wellington public house is on the left where the motor vehicle is parked.

A postcard view of London Road from just below Victoria Park. Picture postcards are a valuable historical record of the past but it was not until 1894 that privately printed postcards could be sent, bearing a halfpenny stamp. One of the first companies in Britain to produce such cards was F.T. Corkett of Leicester. This photograph dates to about 1910.

The Wyvern Hotel dominates this scene as passengers await trams outside the Midland Railway station, pictured here in the 1940s. In 1841 Thomas Cook made his famous excursion from Leicester to Loughborough and a statue of Cook now stands outside the station to commemorate his role as the founding father of the excursion holiday.

The first tram took to the rails in Leicester in 1874 providing a service between the centre of the town and the Belgrave area. Routes along Humberstone Road and London Road began in the following year. Initially, a consortium of two private companies operated the service, but an Act of Parliament in 1870 enabled the Leicester Corporation to assume control of the concession. After a long period of consultation the corporation decided to electrify and extend the system and the new operation began on 18 May 1904.

The posts carrying the electric wires for the trams travelling up London Road here in 1897 have a certain elegance today, as does the uncluttered frontages of the railway station.

In this photograph are examples of three nineteenth-century forms of traction. The horse-drawn carriages are still in evidence, whilst an electric tram approaches from Granby Street, and the internal combustion engine is represented by Bennett's delivery van. The impressive frontage of the Wyvern Hotel provides a fine architectural connection between the Midland Railway station and the shops and businesses in Granby Street.

London Road had all the potential to become a 'gateway' to the city from the south. The entire route as far south as the junction with Granville Road and Evington Road (pictured here in 1897) was formerly known as Gallowtree Gate. The gallows in question stood near this junction at the entrance to the Evington Footpath. The building on the left, Granby House, built in 1876, is still standing, but it has lost its lantern. The church with the spire was formerly Victoria Road Baptist church, and is now a church of the Seventh Day Adventists. This photograph was taken sometime between 1893 (when the station and the Wyvern Hotel were built) and the arrival of the town's electric trams in 1902.

An elegant horse-drawn carriage awaits its passengers in 1893.

This photograph of the Presbyterian church of St Stephen and the Midland Railway station could only have been taken in 1892 or early in 1893 when the railway station had been built. The church was demolished in that year to make way for the building of the Wyvern Hotel. To the rear of the site of the Wyvern Hotel was the Campbell Street station, first used on 4 May 1840. All that remains now of this station is a pair of Egyptian-looking gateposts in Campbell Street.

Midland Railway Station. Leicester.

A view of the façade of the railway station intended for the tourist trade of about 1910. There is an air of elegance in this scene: the electric tram gantries with their wrought ironwork, the rhythm of the station's arcading, and the grandeur of the Wyvern Hotel.

This view from 1967 looking north along platform five of the Great Central Railway station. The photographer, Nigel Tout, has recorded perfectly the emptiness and redundancy of the station. The twelve factory chimneys on the skyline are a reminder of Leicester's past industrial landscape.

five
Parks and
Open Spaces

Abbey Park was opened to the public on Whit Monday 1882 and still reflects Victorian tastes with formal gardens and a bandstand. This is the main entrance in 1897. Abbey Park Road appears unsurfaced and there is no sight of the city's bus depot later constructed there. The park was created from the Abbey Meadows and was acquired by the Corporation in 1876. Barron & Sons of Derby won a competition to design the park.

A view of the entrance from Abbey Park Road taken a few years later. The park has several different landscapes and this eastern section remains relatively open, a popular play area for children. The park was extended in 1925 with the addition of the former Leicester Abbey site, connected to it by a footbridge across the River Soar.

Abbey Park's origins, as the location of the Abbey of St Mary in the Meadow, are still apparent today in its landscape. This photograph was taken shortly after dawn on an autumn day in 1969, the wildlife of the park yet to be disturbed by the urban invaders.

The evocative ruins of Cavendish House in Abbey Park date partly to the 1560s when the buildings of the former abbey were given to Henry Hastings, Earl of Huntingdon. He built a mansion using materials from the abbey, incorporating the original gatehouse. In 1613, the property came into the hands of William Cavendish, first Earl of Devonshire, and during the Civil War it served as the headquarters of Charles I's troops before the battle of Naseby. After the battle the building was burned by royal troops. Some of the ruins still stand and evidence of burning can be seen.

A cycle race in progress near the pavilion in Abbey Park in the 1950s. Horse and equestrian trials were added later to the spectacles as part of the annual City of Leicester Show attracting the country's top riders including HRH Princess Anne. Her great-great-grandfather, Edward VII, opened the park.

Eight weeks before the BBC opened in Leicester, its first local radio station, the Corporation's publicity trailers headed for the city's major annual festival, the City of Leicester Show in Abbey Park. In 1886 the park held its first flower show and gala, an annual event that continued (war years excepted) until 1939. In 1947 the tradition was superseded by the City of Leicester Show, which continued annually until the early 1990s.

Opposite, below: The penny farthing bicycle was invented by James Starley of the Coventry Machinists Company. By increasing the diameter of the front wheel of the existing French 'boneshaker' he gained more speed. The bicycle was so high that it needed a mounting step to reach up to the seat called a hammock saddle. The penny farthing was made entirely of metal, instead of wood and had rubber tyres rather than wooden wheels but the high centre of gravity made them very unstable. This race in Abbey Park took place in around 1890

For landscape historians and researchers this is a most valuable photograph of Abbey Park and dates to the closing years of the nineteenth century. The panoramic view draws in the River Soar, the bridge that connects the two areas of the park and the pavilion. In the distance are the factory chimneys of the St Margaret's area of the town, a reminder that Leicester's industrial heart was never far away.

Abbey Park has seen big crowds, from Jubilee celebrations to Bonfire Night parties, but for most of the time, it is still a quiet place despite being so close to the heart of a busy city. Here, two young girls, with perhaps their nanny, enjoy the peace of the park in around 1920.

Abbey Park gates, 1980. On either side of the wrought iron gates are two Tudor-style lodges designed by James Tait in 1881. The lodge on the left is the more ornate of the two. It is decorated with ornamental crests representing the borough arms. The right-hand building carries a canopied structure that houses the bell once rung at park closing time.

On the last day of 1925 the Earl of Dysart gave 32 acres of land that comprised the abbey grounds to the town council. Seven years later the marshy land had been levelled and a bridge built to connect the new land with the existing park. Nearby Dysart Way was named in honour of the Earl. During the work the foundations of the abbey church were revealed and are now marked out to show the abbey plan. Further refurbishment was undertaken in 2005 following archaeological surveys of the site. This postcard dates from about 1910.

The Lewis gun was designed before the First World War but is seen here being used in anti-aircraft drills on Victoria Park in 1940. The men are an attachment of the Royal Army Ordnance Corps, possibly reservists or Territorial Army. The equipment and some of the clothing date from the First World War but Ordnance Corps were not front line troops, hence the lack of up-to-date equipment.

Opposite, above: The Abbey Park pavilion and some elegant flower borders seen here sometime in the 1920s.

Opposite, below: An unusual site for a park so close to the centre of an expanding town and one that caught the eye of this photographer from the early Edwardian era. Sheep graze on the grass pasture of Victoria Park. The grand houses around the park indicate the high status of this area at that time.

The atmosphere of a racecourse is still present in this view of Victoria Park and its pavilion from the 1890s. Even today, the park is unique among Leicester's open spaces for its tree-lined pathways, leading now towards Leicester University's campus.

Historically, the people of Leicester seem to have demonstrated a loyalty to the monarchy and have marked royal events. On 22 June 1911, to mark the Coronation of King George V and Queen Mary, Leicester staged one of its colourful pageants, not in Abbey Park, which has associations with the monarchy, but in Victoria Park.

Sir Edward Landseer Lutyens designed more than 130 war memorials, cemeteries and cenotaphs including the Leicester cenotaph which was built in 1932, midway along the south-west boundary of Victoria Park, at the summit of a formal avenue that carries the eye from Lancaster Road as the park is approached from the city. Leicester's memorial speaks silently but eloquently of the tragedy of war.

New Walk was created in 1785 and is a unique feature of the city of Leicester. It forms a quiet leafy promenade from Victoria Park to the very heart of the city, uninterrupted by roadways. The path now ends where Leicester is governed and managed, at the New Walk Centre, the home of Leicester City Council. The path follows a similar route out of the old town to that of the Roman Gartree Road. It is seen here after a heavy fall of snow in around 1900.

Opposite, above: Central Leicester benefits greatly from its parks at Spinney Hill, Western Park, Abbey Park and Victoria Park. They have been described as the 'lungs' of the city providing not only pleasant open spaces but also opportunities for recreation and relaxation, sport and contemplation. Railings originally enclosed Victoria Park – today, as in the 1960s when this photograph was taken, it is less formal.

Opposite, below: Leicester's 69-acre Victoria Park opened in 1882 and occupies land that was part of the former South Field of the town. It served as the town's racecourse from 1806 to 1883. Whereas Abbey Park has an atmosphere of antiquity because of its past, Victoria Park has a sense of the countryside despite now being a part of the urban landscape. These low buildings form the entrance from London Road, seen here in 1920.

Leicester's electricity generating station was decommissioned in the 1970s and demolished some twenty years later. The Walker's football stadium now dominates this area. Photographed here in the 1950s, the silhouetted figures give this view of the power station, taken from under the packhorse bridge near Swan Lake Mills, an evocative feel.

six

Lost Buildings

A haunting image from late nineteenth-century Leicester and one that was about to change. The view is looking from Holy Bones into St Nicholas Street, the eastern section of which is now part of modern High Street and the rest is beneath the Southgates underpass and Holiday Inn. Demolition was imminent to make way for the Great Central Railway station and its approach road, constructed between 1898 and 1900. Posters on the windows of Samuel Freeman, furniture dealer, announce a (closing down?) sale, John Pearce, ironmonger and electrical dealer has closed, as has Maria Johnson's bakery and John Wadd's grocers shop. Posters advertise the Tivoli Music Hall in Belgrave Gate.

Opposite, above: The General Newsroom, pictured here in the 1890s, was designed in Greek revival style by the Leicester architect William Flint and was built in Granby Street on the north corner with Belvoir Street in 1838. It was a dramatic-looking building and maybe somewhat out of place amid less classical adjacent buildings. It was used as a reading room and early reference library, though with the atmosphere of a gentlemens' club. It was demolished in 1901 for road widening as Granby Street became the preferred route for traffic entering the town from the London Road.

Opposite, below: A drawing of the General Newsroom. Flint was one of Leicester's most prolific architects. He was born in 1801, the son of a schoolteacher and was articled in 1818 to William Parsons. He was clerk of the works to the building of St George's church in Rutland Street (designed by Parsons) and was appointed Architect and Surveyor to the Borough in 1836. His other work includes the Methodist chapel in Charles Street (1830), the library in Belvoir Street (1831) and Crescent Cottages in King Street (1836).

The late Fred Dibnah, who in his later years became a television personality and industrial historian, was responsible for the demolition of the Co-op Dairy chimney in Glenfield. Leicester, like so many Midland towns and cities, was a forest of factory chimneys until the 1960s and the felling of each one was a community event. The chimney, in many cases, symbolised one's place of work and, more often than not, a place of work strongly influenced or controlled one's way of life.

The demolition of a chimney often meant the closure of a company and the consequent loss of jobs in the nearby dependent community. Sometimes tears were shed when these familiar landmarks fell. The Glenfield Co-op chimney fell during May 1982, using Dibnah's familiar technique of replacing supporting bricks at the base of the chimney with wood, which disintegrated when set on fire.

The photographer chose to emphasise the scale of the Leicestershire Club in Welford Road by adopting a low camera position, so allowing the passers-by to enhance the perspective. As a result, the building has an air of solidity, tradition and – to some extent – anonymity. The building, designed by Joseph Goddard and built in 1876, is still in use today as a place of social activity, and little of the fabric has been altered. It stands adjacent to the modern court buildings and opposite the tower blocks of Leicester City Council's New Walk Centre in Welford Place. This photograph dates to around 1895.

Pictured here at the end of the nineteenth century, the Royal Hotel, between Horsefair Street and the Market Place, which advertised 'hot and cold water in thirty rooms' as well as being 'centrally situated, fully licensed, with a good cuisine'. The formal and elegant frontage dominates the surrounding shops. Next door is E. Blake's tailor and drapery shop, formerly owned by D. Maclean.

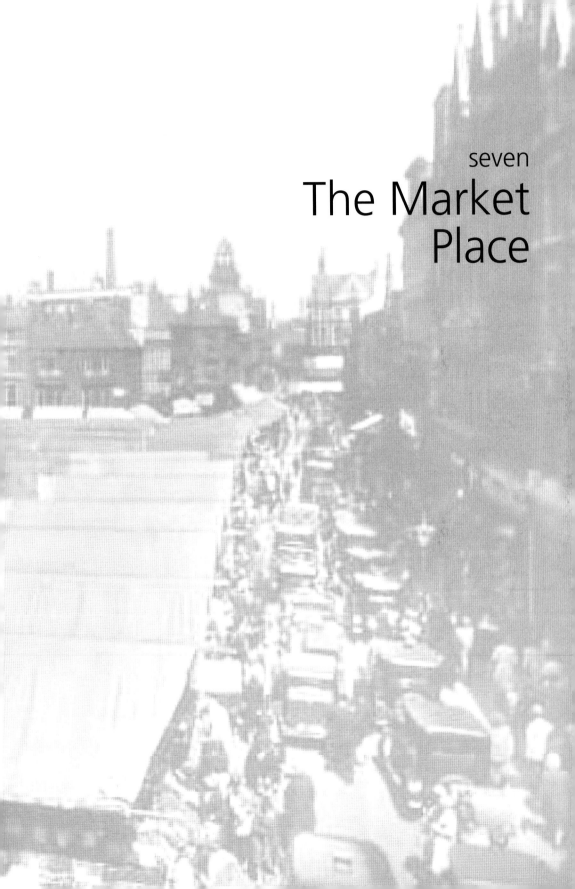

seven

The Market Place

The buildings at the heart of the Market Place adjoining the square have witnessed some colourful events. The first Market Hall in the town was built in 1440 by the Duchy of Lancaster and was known as 'Le Draperie'. Later, the 'Gainsborough' was built. The origins of the name are unknown, but it was operating by 1533 and served as a market hall and a prison. The borough justices met in a first floor room. A newer Gainsborough replaced this in 1747, designed by the Leicester architect John Westley, but demolished in 1851 and rebuilt as a single storey hall to a design by C. Wickes. The Corn Exchange was built in 1855 on the same site, the design by F.W. Ordish, with its remarkable rusticated open bridge and staircase, being the result of a competition held by the corporation. The notice next to the lamppost is an advertisement for a cheese stores. It is thought that this photograph dates to about 1900.

Horsefair Street and Market Approach from a postcard view. The exact date of this photograph is unknown, but it is likely to be around 1910.

The Market Approach pictured here around 1910 was built to celebrate Queen Victoria's Jubilee, as was the clock in the centre of the photograph, which for many years has been known fondly as 'Kemp's Clock'. A number of taverns and shops were demolished to make way for this new entrance to the market, the curve of the façades intended as a way of drawing the eye towards the colourful stalls beyond.

A tour of Leicester's various market places is a tour through the long history of the town, from Cank Street to Loseby Lane, from Cow Lane to Silver Street. The Roman forum was, of course, a place of trading. Later, the butchers sold their meat in the street near St Nicholas' church now known as Holy Bones. Gradually, the Saturday Market grew in importance and became the principal market after the closure of the High Cross Market in the nineteenth century. The awnings above the market stalls suggest a pre-war date for this photograph, probably around 1935.

Corn Exchange, 1971. In more recent times, the Corn Exchange has had an eventful history. After serving as a night club, it was partly gutted by fire. Although a number of schemes were discussed by the City Council including the use of the building as an indoor market, it remained empty until the 1990s. It has now been refurbished and is trading again as public house.

The modern Market Place was formerly the Saturday Market, dating back to 1298, receiving its Royal Charter from Elizabeth I in 1588. Unlike earlier markets, which were located in the central area of the medieval town, the Saturday Market was situated in the town's south-east corner. The statue of the Fifth Duke of Rutland can be seen here in this photograph from about 1898, above and behind the stalls. First erected in 1852 on the site of the ancient Conduit at the opposite end of the Market Place, it was moved to this location twenty years later and stands in this position today, but now faces south, rather than east.

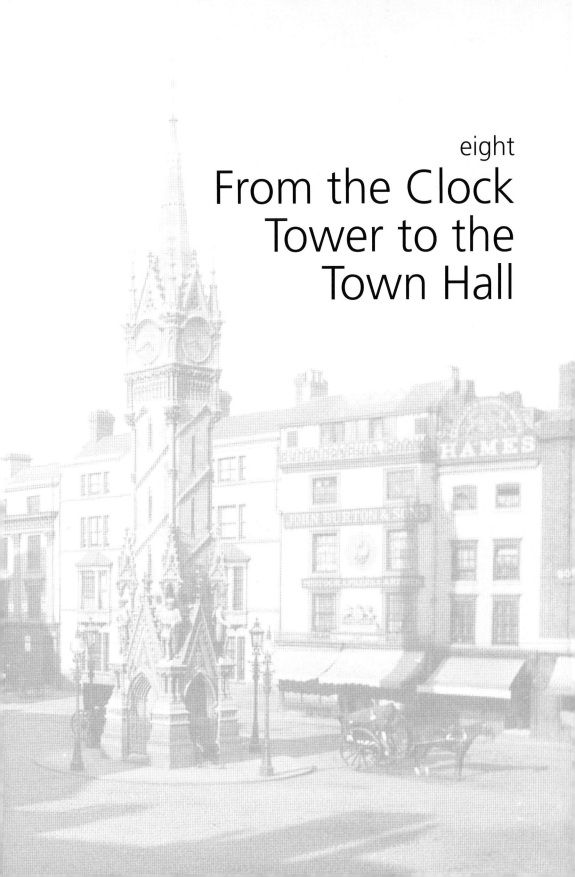

eight

From the Clock Tower to the Town Hall

The Clock Tower stands just outside the eastern boundary of the medieval town, close to the former East Gate. A large building used as assembly rooms and later shops was built near the site in about 1750 and demolished in 1862 to create the open space that remains today. This junction of five roads pictured here around 1905, assumed more importance in the nineteenth century when the route along London Road became Leicester's principal thoroughfare.

A rare view of the 'Eastgates' and the coffee house on the corner of Churchgate. The architect Edward Burgess was responsible for designing all three of Leicester's coffee houses. This view from High Street looking along the Haymarket towards Belgrave Gate is from around 1910. The coffee house, on the left, was built in 1885 with half-timbered gables, and the lead-capped cupola above the ground floor was formerly arcaded with curved oriels.

The Clock Tower, pictured here in about 1910, is a memorial to four of Leicester's historic benefactors, Simon de Montfort, William Wigston, Sir Thomas White and Gabriel Newton. It was designed by the Leicester architect Joseph Goddard and completed at the cost of precisely £1,000. The column of the tower is built of Ketton stone from neighbouring Rutland, statues around the base are of Portland stone and the angled pillars are of granite and serpentine.

Gallowtree Gate, *c.* 1900. Thomas Cook's offices are in the right foreground. On the left is the junction with Humberstone Gate. If the time on the clock is correct, the shops are still trading after five o' clock in the afternoon.

In the shadow of the Clock Tower, and photographed just before the First World War, the remarkably large workforce of M. Johnson & Co. (Provisions Merchants) stands proudly to attention. Meat and poultry is on display, on hooks in the open air, at a time before food hygiene regulations applied.

Miss Watts in her *Walk Through Leicester* of 1804 noted that many new buildings had been built along Granby Street and this new phase of construction probably coincided with the adoption of the new street name (previously Gallowtree Gate). At first, it was just the section from Belvoir Street to London Road but later also included the part up to Horsefair Street. This is the splendid coffee house close to the corner of Rutland Street, senn here in about 1898.

Granby Street, *c.* 1950. A view towards the city centre from the junction of Granby Street and where the modern Central Ring Road (St George's Way) meets London Road.

The Co-op, Union Street, 1884. This imposing mid-nineteenth-century façade is now incorporated into the modern Shires Shopping Development. These 'new' central stores and offices for the Leicester Co-operative Society Ltd were designed by Thomas Hind and are depicted here in an architect's lithograph of the time. Mr B. Hemmings, president of the Society, opened it on 10 November 1894.

Trams and horse-drawn carts travel sedately along Granby Street. This view from around 1900 is towards the junction with Horsefair Street.

An old image from about 1920 showing the hustle and bustle in Humberstone Gate. All these buildings are now long gone. The Haymarket Shopping Precinct occupies the entire length of the road from the Clock Tower to Charles Street and it is now pedestrianised.

From at least as early as the mid-eighteenth century, Leicester's retail centre began moving away from the High Street towards the roads radiating from the Clock Tower. This photograph has all the atmosphere of a typical day in the life of a street devoted to retail trade and probably dates to around 1900. Beyond the Clock Tower can be seen the premises of M. Johnson & Co.

Local architect F.J. Hames built Leicester's Town Hall between 1874 and 1876 to a very pleasing design. Built of deep red Suffolk brick with dressings of Ketton stone, it is without doubt one of the most delightful civic structures in the area. *The Builder*, published on 5 June 1897, described it as 'quiet good taste, conveying a sense of civic dignity and pride without being too grandiose or monumental'. It was opened by the Mayor of Leicester, Ald. William Kempson, on 3 August 1874. The date of this photograph is not known, but would appear to be from around the turn of the nineteenth/twentieth centuries.

The fountain and memorial in Town Hall Square, in the first decade of the twentieth century. Built on part of the former Horse Fair site, the Town Hall with its adjacent square is to scale and in harmony with its surroundings. The ground slopes away to the north of the site, but the balance of the building has been maintained by locating the clock tower at the northern end. This view is from the junction of Every Street and Bishop Street.

An early photograph of Town Hall Square from 1896, the fountain and the Town Hall in the background. This is another example of a 'candid' approach to photography. The photographer was not interested in the buildings except in using them as a backdrop for the people who are engaged in animated conversation, apparently oblivious of him.

nine

Shops and Services

Charnwood Street was once a thriving shopping area. J.K. Wilkinson founded the Wilkinson household retail chain here in 1930. Even in the 1950s, butchers, drapers, breweries, hairdressers, pastry cooks, bakers and 'Paddy's Swag Store' were still here. This off-license and stores on the corner with Vulcan Road, Shipstones Off Sales, was photographed in 1934. The shop sold beer, but not wines or spirits, and all manner of groceries and tobacco. Local people remember buying sugar in the thick blue paper bags and eggs for one penny each. The licensee was Charles Barrington and on the front door is a poster for *On the Dole* showing at the Palace Theatre. Just opposite was Leicester's Ansells Brewery.

M.E. Bower's shop, 23 Belvoir Street in 1873. The most famous Leicester shop name on the wall of 23 Belvoir Street is that of Simpkin and James who were to be found at the junction of the Market Place and Horsefair Street. Perhaps Mr Bower once worked for them before he set out on his own as a shopkeeper.

Above: J. Winterhalder's shop window in Belgrave Gate, *c.* 1898. A true glimpse into the past. The passer-by is oblivious of the photographer, though the young man in the doorway is obviously posing and is presumably the proprietor.

Left: Shops in London Road, on the corner of Highfield Street, just south of the railway station, *c.* 1896.

Haymarket Shopping Centre, Christmas. 1980. For many years, the culmination of Leicester's charitable 'Toys on the Table' appeal, organised by Leicester Lions and supported by various media organisations, was this cascade of toys and presents in the central areas of the Haymarket Shopping Centre.

Opposite, above: The construction of the central ring road, the Southgates Underpass and St Nicholas Circle in the 1960s required the demolition of an area of medieval Leicester. Streets that respected the Roman grid pattern were destroyed, including Redcross Street, the location of one of Leicester's earliest markets, and a view of Applecross Street between Bath Lane and Talbot Lane. Here, George Glover is standing outside his shop in Applegate Street in about 1910. Next door at No.7 is Ferneyhough & Sons, printers.

Opposite, below: Wharf Street in the nineteenth and twentieth centuries was a community within a community – strong local identity and community spirit despite hardships. Along the length of this street was every type of shop and business. This photograph from 1934 is of the A-1 Meat Company, located opposite the old Hippodrome Theatre. The proprietor in the white apron, holding a child, is Bill Sturgess and his assistant, also in an apron, is Frank Jarman. The occasion was an annual Christmas event when toys to the value of £150 – a large amount for that time – were handed out to local children. A policeman has been assigned to the event and can be seen just below the gas lamp. Next door, at No. 20 is William Ronald Smith's fish shop. There is a cycle shop on the edge of the picture at the corner of Fleet Street offering bicycle hire at three pennies per day.

Joseph Johnson of Market Street, on the corner of Belvoir Street (pictured here around 1897) advertised themselves as 'complete outfitters for ladies, gentlemen and children. Drapers, furnishers, ladies hairdressers and restauranteurs'. The building, framed by Market Street, Belvoir Street and Bowling Green Street is now occupied by the department store, Fenwick's.

Walter E. Sturgess set up his shop on the corner of Cranmer Street and Shaftsbury Road, just off the Narborough Road, in 1897. As well as making, selling and repairing bicycles, Walter designed his own cane work bicycle trailers, some of which are visible in the photograph. He spent a short time in Australia before establishing his business which might have something to do with the name of the trailer, called 'Austral'. His business prospered and he moved to new premises in nearby Narborough Road then to Braunstone Gate. From bicycles, he moved onto motorcycles and then motor cars. Today, Sturgess is one of the largest Nissan dealerships in the UK and is still a family business.

ten
Worship

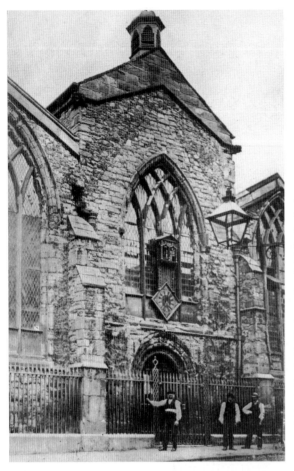

All Saints church, with its still surviving automaton clock located above the porch of the church. This is a rare photograph of the West front of the church with its Norman doorway before its restoration. The seventeenth-century clock, with its quaint Jacobean figures, was restored in 1899-1900 but the old movement was discarded. The clock was moved to the South entrance of the church after the restoration. Sadly, both jacks were stolen in the early 1980s, when the church became redundant, but appear to be present in this photograph that dates from 1856. A re-creation of this clock has been made by local horologist Colin Clarke and is on display in the inner courtyard of the Guildhall.

Belgrave Hall, Belgrave House and the Church of St Peter's form an oasis of calm close to busy traffic routes. This is a picture of the nave and choir of St Peter's taken in 1873.

Holy Cross Priory, Wellington Street, 1873. The first introduction of the English Dominicans to the Roman Catholic diocese of Nottingham was at Hinckley, where for many years they served Leicester. Their mission at Leicester was put on a permanent basis in 1798 by the purchase of a house by Father Francis Xavier Choppelle. The present church of the Holy Cross in Wellington Street was begun by Father Benedict Caestrick in 1815 and opened in 1819.

The church of St Paul in Dale Street on the corner of Melbourne Road, 1896. It was built by the Methodists of the New Connexion to replace a former chapel near London Road railway station that closed in 1890. Between 1965 and 2000 it was the home of the Polish Catholic Church in Leicester. A Polish Community in Leicester was founded in 1948 following settlement of Polish soldiers and their families after the war who organised themselves into an active community. Fr Frackowiak, an army chaplain, was seconded to Leicester so that they could celebrate Holy Mass in their mother tongue. After a period of fundraising, enough money was raised to purchase this church and on 12 June 1965 Bishop Władysław Rubin and Bishop Edward Ellis of Nottingham performed the consecration.

St Nicholas' church is Leicester's oldest surviving place of worship and may have been built on the site of a Roman temple. Two small windows in the north wall of the nave date from the Saxon period and were constructed using Roman tiles. By the end of the seventeenth century the church had lost its spire and by 1825 was in poor condition and threatened with demolition, but was fortunately rescued by a major restoration project.

A remarkable building stands on the corner of St Peter's Road and Melbourne Road in the Highfields. Melbourne Hall, pictured here in 1897, has its roots in the England of the Restoration. Its founder, the Baptist minister, Dr F.B. Meyer, one of the most influential Free Church bible teachers of the first half of the twentieth century, requested that the building should be designed in the shape of a lantern to signify the desire to bring the light of the 'good news' of salvation in Jesus Christ to the people of Leicester. It is an evangelical Free Church. Meyer's preaching often attracted more than 800 worshippers to each service.

Right: St Mark's church in Belgrave Gate, pictured here in about 1920, was built in 1870-2 of Charnwood slate with a red brick-lined interior. The tower and slender spire rise to a height of 168ft. The vicar, Canon Frederick Donaldson was a radical social reformer who for ten years led a group of Christian Socialists and attracted thousands to his soap-box sermons in Leicester's market. St Mark's became redundant as its parish became more commercial and less residential. After several failed attempts the church has now been rescued from decay and has benefited from responsible refurbishment.

Below: It is said that Geoffrey Chaucer was married here, in the church of St Mary de Castro, to Philippa de Root, sister of Katherine, mistress and subsequently third wife of John of Gaunt.

The church of St George was built between 1823 and 1837 to a design by the County Surveyor William Parsons and was the first new church to be built in the borough since the Middle Ages. The decision to build it reflected the growth in population in the area in the first part of the nineteenth century. It was erected on land that formed part of the glebe of St Margaret's. The church was almost ruined by a fire on 5 October 1911 and this rare picture recorded the catastrophic event.

Albion Street, stretching away into the distance from its Dover Street junction, with the Black Boy public house just visible, and on the right, the York Street Gospel Hall, *c.* 1980. On the far right of the picture is part of Pick's Knitwear factory. The small chapel on the corner of Dover Street was demolished in the 1990s and replaced by an apartment block.

The rebuilding of St George's, after the fire of 1911, began in 1913, directed by W.D. Caroe. The nave was totally lost in the fire and the tower and chancel both required heavy restoration. Here the church footpath is seen in the 1980s, prior to more recent refurbishment.

St George's church, *c.* 1980. It has for some time been the Leicester home of the Serbian Orthodox church and in the early part of the twenty-first century has received further restoration, with funding from English Heritage and Leicester City Council including the rebuilding of the retaining walls to the churchyard. It stands at the centre of an area being developed as the city's new cultural quarter.

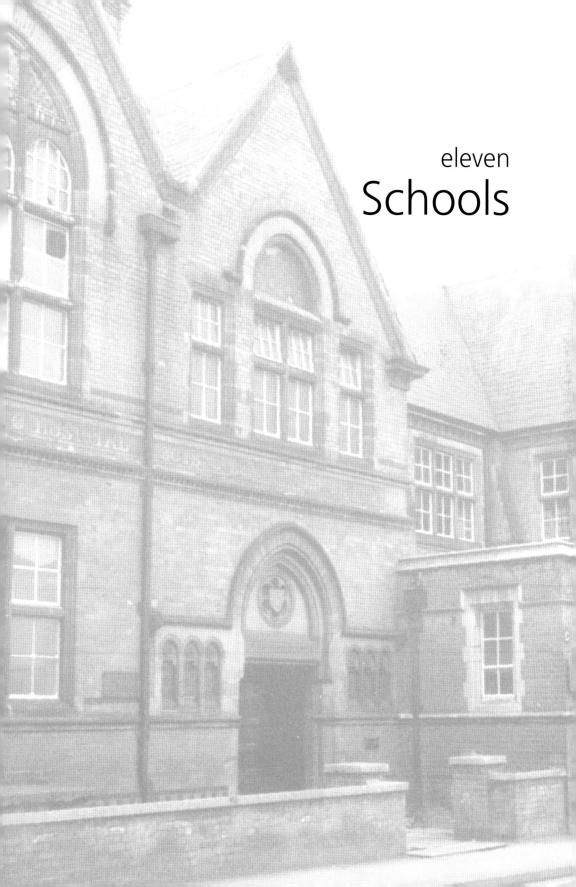

eleven

Schools

In the later half of the nineteenth century, the old Wyggeston Foundation almost ceased to exist, at least for providing schooling. In 1873 a new school for boys was founded, using funds accrued from the trust's land investments. The Revd James Went was appointed headmaster and a new building was opened in 1877 in High Cross Street, close to the old Wyggeston Hospital. In 1920, the school transferred to new accommodation on land near Victoria Park, adjacent to the present Leicester University where the buildings now serve as a sixth-form college. The High Cross Street buildings later accommodated the Alderman Newton's Boys' School, and were purchased in 1980 by the Leicester Grammar School Trust. For many years, remains of the retaining walls of the old hospital were visible in the playground, adjacent to the cathedral precincts, but these were covered over when re-surfacing took place in the 1990s. The buildings have extensive rooms below the street level that have been used in recent times as changing rooms. No doubt because of its proximity to the St Martin's graveyard there are persistent reports of ghostly appearances in the area.

Opposite, above: The former Wyggeston Hospital Girls' School and sometime City of Leicester Boys' School in Humberstone Gate pictured here soon after its completion in 1878. Education in Leicester was provided first by the Abbey of St Mary in the Meadows, but for over four centuries the provision was strongly influenced by the foundation established by William Wigston – a wealthy merchant – and his brother Thomas Wigston, a canon at the Newarke College.

Opposite, below: The new home of the Wyggeston Girls' School was designed by Symington & Prince and constructed on land that was formerly part of the great South Field. When it opened in 1928 there were 683 pupils on the roll. This photograph was taken just prior to the first term at the school, with construction vehicles and equipment still evident. The building is now the location of Regent College.

The Wyggeston Hospital Girls' School was built in 1878 on Humberstone Gate between Hill Street and Clarence Street. The first headmistress was Miss Ellen Leicester who, with four assistant mistresses, taught 150 pupils. The school roll grew and a new building was constructed on Regent Road in 1928. The original building served as an educational establishment for many years and is now the headquarters of Age Concern Leicester. This photograph was taken in 1984.

A variety of architectural styles from differing periods could be seen in Humberstone Gate in 1980. The former Wyggeston Hospital Girls' School is now partially hidden by more modern shop frontages and dwarfed by the high-rise building further along the road.

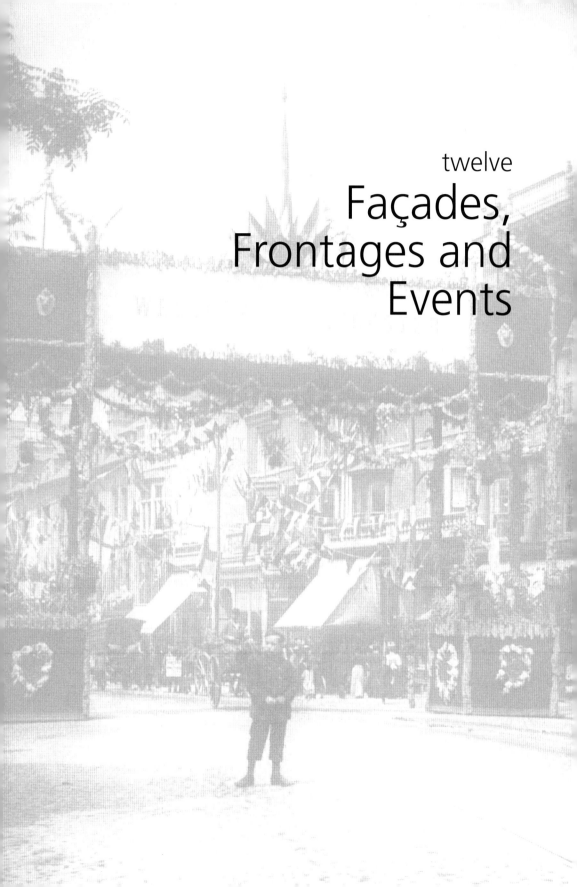

twelve

Façades, Frontages and Events

Left: No. 17 Friar Lane (from about 1920) standing on a quiet street that even in the twenty-first century has retained its elegance. When, in 1845, a suitable location for a new Town Hall was sought, a site in Friar Lane was one of the options considered.

Opposite above: The Spa, Humberstone Gate, 1913. Four large, brick houses were built around 1793 following identification of a local mineral spring. Watts, in her *Walk through Leicester* describes them and adds that 'though furnished by the proprietor with neat marble baths and every convenient appendage for bathing' the spring was 'not found sufficiently impregnated with mineral properties to bring it into use'. The venture failed and the building was used as a General Baptist college from 1793 that closed around 1860. The building was later converted into four separate residences.

Left: Friar Lane is named after the Franciscan friary. The road is first mentioned in the Wyggeston Hospital Charters in 1391, though it was in existence before that time. No. 17 Friar Lane was described by Professor Jack Simmons as 'the most handsomest Georgian house left in the old town'.

Opposite, below: The Surgeon's House, New Walk, 1913. For a time the promenade of New Walk marked the limit of residential building development to the south-west. Today there is a diversity of houses, businesses and places of worship along the route but in previous times, living in New Walk conferred status and it was reserved mainly for those occupied in the professions. This house at the time belonged to Charles Crossley, a surgeon.

The architect Edward Burgess was responsible for many of Leicester's finest Victorian buildings and the Liberal Club in Bishop Street is one of his designs. This building is now Alliance House and the ground floor façade is replaced by a hotchpotch of modern shop frontages. This view from about 1898 is from Every Street, with Town Hall Square to the right. The retaining wall in the foreground, on the left of the picture, is the rear of the HSBC bank.

The Liberal Club in Bishop Street (originally Bishopgate) forms one side of Town Hall Square, a civic open space created from the site of the early horse and cattle market when that was transferred to part of the Freemens' Common. This view from 1897 is along Granby Street.

Granby Street, 1897. This important route was widened in 1868, which resulted in the demolition of several buildings, including the Newsroom, at the corner of Belvoir Street and Granby Street. However, a number of new buildings of great quality were built in the following years such as Joseph Goddard's Midland Bank (right), a remarkable blend of Gothic and Oriental styles, built in 1870-1872.

Leicester's voluntary hospital, later the Royal Leicester Infirmary, was founded in Oxford Street in 1771 and was maintained by voluntary contributions. The person near the lamppost was evidently moving too fast to be caught by the camera – long exposure times were required at the time. One wonders why the photographer, working in about 1899, chose this particular angle, emphasising the uniform nature of the façade of the building, rather than focusing on the entrance which can just be seen on the far right.

Left: Meadows Distillery poster. This building on the corner of Humberstone Gate and Clarence Street is one of the most satisfying examples of a Victorian shop front in the city centre. Built as a warehouse for wines and spirits it was, in more recent years, occupied by Greens, the electrical retailer, but now, following several changes of occupier, is looking sadly run-down.

Below: The original architect's drawing for the Meadows Distillery in Humberstone Gate. The wine and spirits merchants Challis and Allen later used the buildings, whilst the adjacent shops (Nos 40-42 Humberstone Gate) have housed several businesses trading as hosiers and outfitters.

Charles Street police station was closed in 2004. This picture can be dated with some accuracy to the mid-1980s by the high-rise office block in the background (on Humberstone Gate) and the configuration of the road and railings that were altered in the 1990s. The two lamps on the top of the building, either side of the flagstaff, date to the time of Chief Constable O.J.B. Cole (1929-1955). One was red and the other green. If the red one was lit, it indicated that there had been a fatal road traffic accident. If the green lamp was lit, then all was well. The building is now central to the business and cultural regeneration scheme for the St George's area of the city.

An interesting example of a building designed to fit a difficult location. This former General Accident, Fire and Life Assurance Building is in Wellington Street although the postal address is 2 King Street and the building faces Belvoir Street! The photograph dates from around 1960. In more recent times it was used as a social club for Leicester City Council employees and is now the 'Original 4' nightclub, boasting no less than four floors offering different musical styles.

Above: A panorama of architectural styles along Humberstone Gate to the junction with Charles Street, pictured here in 1978. Prominent in the centre of the photograph is the former Meadows Distillery, an architect's drawing of which can be seen on page 110. To the right is the mock-Tudor gatehouse of the former Wyggeston School and to the left, on the opposite side of Charles Street, is the Haymarket Shopping Centre.

Right: West Bridge, *c.* 1980. Possibly, no English monarch has caused such emotive feelings in Leicester as Richard III. West Bridge is the location of the often-told story of the foretelling of Richard's fate at Bosworth Field.

The Talbot Inn on Thurcaston Road by the side of the River Soar in the heart of Old Belgrave in 1873. The building has since lost its upper storey and the old elm tree is now gone. Older residents of Belgrave remember a covered area in the pub's yard where they played as children and a spot nearby where they watched horses pulling barges on the towpath along the river.

The Freemen's Hotel in 1898, which stands on the corner of Aylestone Road and Knighton Street, on the route between the Filbert Street football ground and the city centre. The proprietor was Mr E. Clayton. The hotel name reflects the close proximity of the Freemen's Common on the ancient South Field of the town. Posters advertise a Fosse Sports firework display at the County Cricket Ground and a forthcoming match between Aylestone and Fosse. Leicester Fosse club was formed in 1884, moved to the Filbert Street ground in 1891, entered the football league in 1894 and became Leicester City in 1912. The football club shared the County Cricket Ground for a while before the acquisition of Filbert Street.

Opposite: This alley, a narrow turning off Guildhall Lane, is close to the Guildhall and the cathedral and is known as Coronation Place. It leads to a small cobbled lane that runs along the rear of properties fronting High Street. It is pictured here in the 1970s.

Near to better known buildings of grander scale and design is this charming original frontage in New Street. The symmetry of the design gives an air of quiet respectability and confidence, no doubt the qualities that the office clerks inside were also required to live up to. The frontage has changed very little since this photograph was taken in the early 1970s.

This fine Victorian building in Horsefair Street survives today. It faces Town Hall Square and on the right hand side of the building can be seen the footpath that still exists, connecting Horsefair Street and the Market Place. The building is now a bank providing all the facilities of twenty-first-century banking, yet every aspect of its façade has been retained. The only loss since this photograph was taken over a century ago is the line of low railings at the front of the first floor balcony. The buildings on either side have both been demolished. The rear of this building now adjoins the Victorian fish market, a significant Victorian structure retained and refurbished by Leicester City Council after the fishmongers were relocated to the Market Centre.

Leicester prepares a right-royal welcome, possibly for the visit of King George V and Queen Mary on 10 June 1919. On the right near the street dressings are the premises of Baines and Whitmore. Their trading addresses in Leicester were in Halford Street and London Road, but this view appears to be neither location.

The growth of hotels, from inns and public houses, was closely associated with the turnpiking of the routes into Leicester. Later, the railway age prompted the construction of grand buildings providing a standard of comfort and service previously unknown. The Granville Hotel, seen here in about 1897, was one of those enterprises, serving the newly mobile population, and creating employment for many local people who worked in the service industries such as food and laundry.

The Free Library (*c.* 1898) is still Leicester's lending library, situated on the corner of Belvoir Street and Wellington Street. Most of the façade facing Wellington Street has been rebuilt and a new entrance has been added on Belvoir Street in keeping with the original style.

Above: The last Humberstone Fair, *c.* 1907. There were fairs in Leicester from the thirteenth century, at varying times of the year, but over time these coalesced into two main annual events in May and early October. Humberstone Gate was 'the May' fair with attractions stretching along both sides of the wide street. It is said that Mary Jane Merrick, while pregnant with her son Joseph, was frightened and injured by a parading elephant at a fair in 1862. Joseph later developed physical deformities that led him to be called the 'Elephant Man'.

Left: New Street was so named because it was created at a later date than the surrounding streets (1711), cutting through the area formally occupied by the Greyfriars Priory. This print is from an original by T.D. Newham, published by H. & A. Bennett in Leicester before the First Word War.

Nowhere in Leicester is there a less successful marriage of old and new than in the area of St Nicholas Circle and the Southgates underpass, seen here in about 1980. West Bridge is a site of major historical significance, marking the western boundary of the old town and a site linked with the famous legend of Richard III and the Battle of Bosworth Field. Yet today the bridge is overwhelmed by brutal, concrete-based structures that were the compromise option to an original scheme for the area.

A further panorama of Humberstone Gate in about 1980, with two office block developments of the 1960s evident at the end of Clarence Street. The ten-storey block on the left is Epic House, its roof completely devoid of the forest of communication transmitters and receivers that adorn it today. To its right on the opposite side of Lower Hill Street is Crown House. Obscuring the view of Epic House is the Citadel of the Leicester Central Corps of the Salvation Army on the corner of Kildare Street and Clarence Street.

Opposite, above: Cathedral Square, *c.* 1985. When the adjacent Wyggeston School became redundant in the 1980s, demolition was considered to create a new open vista for the cathedral and its precincts but Leicester Grammar School eventually occupied the buildings. The existing churchyard on the Peacock Lane side of the cathedral was re-landscaped with the addition of a fountain and the realignment of some of the headstones.

Opposite, below: The Judge's Lodgings and adjacent archway leading to the castle are obscured in this view of St Mary de Castro from about 1900, which shows clearly the several phases of building of the church.

The weighbridge toll collector's house (*c.* 1980) in the centre of Humberstone Gate is a delightful building of great character, which has survived despite so much redevelopment around it. Today it is used as the office of a taxi operator. It was built in 1867 on the site of the town's last Haymarket and remained in operation until 1965. The weighbridge itself could handle loads of up to twenty-five tons.

The Welford Road prison was built to resemble a medieval castle and has the highest walls of any prison in Britain. It was built in 1825, the Gatehouse pictured here in 1898 being the earliest structure, replacing a number of ancient and very inadequate gaols in Highcross Street. There have been several extensions and refurbishments.

The Market Square in front of the famous 'bridge of sighs' has been a meeting place for centuries. Ramsay MacDonald spoke here, the Salvation Army have played and sung here and the citizens of Leicester have gathered in the square on innumerable occasions to hear important announcements. This crowd gathered in 1936 to hear the proclamation of the accession of King George VI.

New Walk, looking towards De Montfort Street, 1908. Leicester's popular New Walk seldom appears so deserted so perhaps this photograph was taken early in the day.

The Grand Union Canal, *c.* 1955. A view of the canal looking north-east from near the Frog Island bridge. The buildings in the distance on the curve of the canal are part of the former St Margaret's works of Nathaniel Corah. The modern St Margaret's Way now cuts across this view.

Other local titles published by Tempus

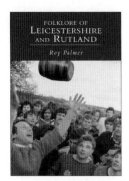

Folklore of Leicestershire and Rutland

ROY PALMER

This book is a comprehensive survey, drawing on a wide range of printed, manuscript and oral material. The topics covered include local legend and lore, ghosts and witchcraft, folk medicine, work and play, sport and fairs, crime and punishment, music, drama and calendar customs in the counties of Leicestershire and Rutland. Roy Palmer is a long-standing member of the English Folk Dance and Song Society and the Folklore Society.

0 7524 2468 8

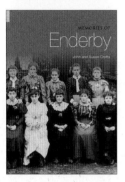

Memories of Enderby

JOHN AND SUSAN CROFTS

This book is a fascinating collection of reminiscences by people who lived or worked in Enderby. There are personal memories of schooldays, childhood games, working life and war years. This is community history at its best.

0 7524 3373 3

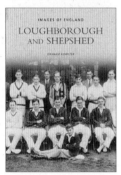

Loughborough and Shepshed

GRAHAM KEMPSTER

This collection of over 180 photographs and other ephemera, drawn from the *Loughborough Echo* archive, traces some of the changes and developments that have taken place in Loughborough and Shepshed during the last 120 years. From Coronation celebrations in 1902 and the construction of Loughborough post office in 1930 to Shepshed Parade and Gala in 1950, each image recalls the social history of the area.

0 7524 3252 4

Nuneaton Volume II

PETER LEE

This absorbing collection provides a nostalgic glimpse into the history of Nuneaton during the last century. Compiled with over 160 photographs and postcards, this selection highlights some of the changes and events that have taken place in the town. From glimpses of working life, including cotton, textiles and engineering industries, through to the modernisation of the town during the 1950s and '60s, each image recalls the social history of Nuneaton.

0 7524 3242 7

If you are interested in purchasing other books published by Tempus, or in case you have difficulty finding any Tempus books in your local bookshop, you can also place orders directly through our website

www.tempus-publishing.com